She Who Watches

Willa Holmes

She Who Watches

told by WILLA HOLMES

illustrations by ANDERSON BENALLY

foreword by EVANS GUS KAHCLAMAT

Binford & Mort Publishing
Portland, Oregon

She Who Watches

Copyright © 1997 by Willa Holmes

Printed in the United States of America

Library of Congress Catalog Card Number: 97-74243
ISBN: 0-8323-0520-0

First Edition 1997

Pronunciation Key

Wishram is a very difficult language. Although in the early 1900s it was written down phonetically, it is not commonly spoken today. Perhaps this is how these words were pronounced.

Tsagaglalal	Say-ah-gahg'-lah-lah (Chief of the Wishram)
Celilo	Su-lie'-lo (Celilo Falls once a part of the Columbia River)
Wishram	Wixk-rum (a band of Chinook Indians)
Nixlu'idix	Nix-lu'-i-dix (the Wishram village)
Me'nait	Mu-na'-it (a young fisherman)
Anewi'kus	A-new'-i-kus (an old woman of the village)
Itkla'uwan	It-kla'-u-wan (salmon)
Wi'mahl	Wy'mall (Great River; the Columbia River)

Evans "Gus" Kahclamat

Foreword

My name is Evans Kahclamat. I was born March 2, 1935 at Spearfish, Washington along the Columbia River, at the residence of my grandfather, Oscar Charley Kahclamat, about three hundred yards from "She Who Watches." My ancestors lived for many thousands of years in this area. We speared, netted and trapped fish which we traded to other Western tribes. We had to leave our land with the construction of The Dalles Dam around 1956.

I spent most of the next forty years of my life in the Seattle area—as a surveyor, barber, social service agent, instructional assistant and teacher of cultural arts.

In 1995, I retired from the Seattle School District and moved to Dallesport, Washington, close to my birthplace.

On behalf of my family, I would like to thank Willa Holmes for the effort, research, time and concern she has shown in this publication. Our legends and landmarks are an important part of our history; as a child, they were an essential part of our everyday lives. The beliefs, spirituality, religions, and self-motivation that our people possess are the reasons we have survived many hard years in this area. Thank you, Willa, for a job well done.

Evans "Gus" Kahclamat

Introduction

"She Who Watches," a petroglyph scratched into a pillar of rock overlooking the Columbia River, is one of the most striking and beautiful examples of Native American rock art in the Pacific Northwest. It is also special because it is tied to the old story of Coyote, the trickster, and Tsagaglalal, woman chief of the Wishram band of Chinook who lived there.

The story says Tsagaglalal lived in the village of Nixlu'idix near where the then turbulent Columbia River crashed over Celilo Falls on its way to the sea. Then Coyote came upriver and changed things.

These stories were told by "the oldest of the old" of the Wishram people to Edward Curtis, photographer and chronicler of Native Americans, and to Edward Sapir, anthropologist. They did an invaluable service in translating and saving them for future generations.

ONCE, IN THE TIME BEFORE MEMORIES, Tsagaglalal, woman chief of the Wishram, arose in the darkness just before dawn. She stood on a low bluff above her village, Nixlu'idix, on the northern bank of the Great River. Tsagaglalal pulled an elk skin close about her against the cool fall air. As first morning light turned the sky to a leaden gray, she heard the mournful howl of a coyote on a ridge behind her. A chorus of calls went up in answer: Ah-hoo-o-o . . . Ah-hoo-o-o . . . Ah-hoo-o-o. Shivers ran up her arms. Sometimes when coyotes talked to each other, unexpected things happened.

Shafts of sunlight broke through the clouds and lit the rock walls of the river gorge. In the village below, Tsagaglalal saw her people come, one by one, from their cedar plank longhouses and walk toward the river. Their feet crunched in the early frost on dried grasses. Time had come to carry out plans for winter.

As Tsagaglalal stood on her rock, welcoming the day, a stranger slipped into the village. The figure was wrapped from head to foot in a bearskin as though against a cold East Wind. A young fisherman, Me'nait, saw him first. "Do you come to trade?" he asked. "White Salmon comes soon. We will have many baskets of dried fish for trading. What do you bring?"

"All in good time," the visitor said, his voice muffled by the robe. "But first I would ask you about your village. Do you live well?"

Me'nait nodded.

"Tell me, do you have a good chief?"

Me'nait drew back. This was not like any other trader he had seen and such questions troubled him. Other men of the village gathered around the stranger as a show of strength. They tried to peer under the bearskin, the better to see the outsider, but his face was hidden in shadow.

One of the elders stepped forward. "Our chief is Tsagaglalal. She is wise and firm and kind. We have no quarrel with her."

The others pressed in closer. If the intruder meant them harm, he would know they were ready to defend themselves.

The figure drew back even further into his bearskin. "Take me to your chief," he said. He pointed to Me'nait. "You. Lead the way."

Me'nait looked around at the other men.

"We will go up the trail with you," the elder told him. "Show the stranger the way."

Single file, they made their way across the field strewn with boulders and up into the rocks where Tsagaglalal stood on a wide stone ledge. When they came to the trail below her, Me'nait called up, "Chief Tsagaglalal, this stranger asks to speak with you. Shall I let him come, or should I send him away?"

Chief Tsagaglalal gazed down on the shrouded figure. "Let him come."

"Should we come up also?"

"Return to the river. I will call if I need you."

Me'nait looked back over his shoulder at the stranger. "Someone will be close by," he warned.

Tsagaglalal peered at the figure climbing the rough path, but the stranger stayed close to the rocks and she saw only his shadow. Still, there was something about him that drifted toward her like a whisper of cold air brushing against her cheek.

"Do you not know me?" he asked.

Again coyotes called in the distance and again a strange feeling came to the chief. She remembered when she was a little girl seeing her grandmother tip her head to one side and listen to the coyotes. "Someone in the village will die," the old grandmother would mutter. "Remember, I said it. Soon someone will die."

Tsagaglalal looked at the figure standing just below her. She pulled the elk skin close about her so he would not see her shiver.

He asked again, "Do you not know me?"

"I hear your brothers calling you. Are you one of the Old Ones? Are you the one known as Coyote?"

"That is what I am called."

She thought of the many stories told of Coyote around the campfire. Her people held all of the Old Ones in high regard, but they had many different tales about Coyote. They were in awe of him as Transformer, the one who could change himself or others into many different forms. It was Coyote who could bring change to the life of the People and who taught them new ways. But on winter nights, close by the fire, grandparents also told stories of the Old Ones who lived in this land before the Wishram, her people, came to be. Tales of Coyote's comical antics brought howls of laughter from the children huddled around the fire. His foolish behavior made the older ones smile behind their hands, lest he see. They searched the faces of strangers for him, for he was known to use many disguises.

Tsagaglalal straightened her back and stood tall. He would see from her finely woven basket hat and her soft elk robe she was a respected chief. She spoke to him, allowing no fear to sound in her voice. "How do you come to me? As a leader of the People or as the trickster who often tricks himself?"

Coyote made a soft sound that might have been a laugh. She trembled, sensing power in him, and not feeling as brave as she had sounded.

"It is true," he said, "I trick those who are foolish or need to be taught a lesson. It is also so I sometimes trick the People for my own amusement." He hesitated. "And all too often I end by tricking myself." Then he snorted. She was sure he told the truth. It was indeed Coyote.

He took another step to the top of the path and stood before her, but still she could not see his face within the bearskin. His voice became more pleasant. "Was it not I that gave the People salmon in the river?"

"My people tell such a tale," she said.

"How do the Wishram say it happened?"

She told him this story passed down by grandmothers and grandfathers of years gone past:

4

ONCE, LONG AGO, Coyote walked along Great River, which at that time had no fish in it. Coyote knew the People would soon come to live along the river and would need fish to eat. He spied two women in a canoe who were collecting driftwood in the river. He quickly transformed himself into a broken tree limb and put himself onto the water, for Coyote was able to do such things. He wanted them to pick him up and take him to their home where the women kept many large fish in a lake.

But although he, as a piece of driftwood, bobbed along with the current and floated quite near their canoe, they did not get hold of him. He did not give up. He went ashore, ran ahead along the river and transformed himself into a baby boy. He put himself into a cradle and floated out into the water again. The women heard him wailing and thought he must have come from a canoe that had overturned in the river.

Although the older woman cautioned against it, the younger one took the child and put him into their canoe. "We have not finished gathering driftwood," the older one complained. The younger woman, who longed to have a child of her own, said, "Come now, is it not good to have a boy of our own? Finding a boy is better than finding driftwood." Finally the older one agreed and they took him to their home next to the lake, roasted an eel over the campfire and gave it to him to eat. Then they went on their way again, this time to dig camus roots and gather berries.

Coyote, the crafty one, waited until they were out of sight and changed himself from a baby boy back into his own form. He examined the lake carefully and discovered a spot where he could make an outlet into the river.

He said to himself, "Here I shall make the fish escape from the lake, and they will go into Great River." He made five digging-sticks out of the trunks of young oak trees, for five is the sacred number. He stuck one of his diggers into the ground, braced himself and pulled back. The earth between the lake and the river loosened, but his digging-stick splintered. With a mighty stroke he plunged another digging stick into the ground, and the earth quivered and shook. The channel he was digging grew deeper, but the next strong oak sapling broke into many pieces. Again and again, he stuck a digger into the ground. Then, with all his strength, he forced the last digging stick into the earth. He pried free a huge boulder and water from

the lake roared out into the river with a sound like a clap of thunder. All the fish in the lake were flung into Great River.

When the women came back, they saw what he had done and they knew he was Coyote. "This day, you have treated us badly," they told him. "We were kind to you. We took you in, but you hardened your heart against us. You stole all our fish."

Coyote scolded them. "By what right would you two keep the fish to yourselves?" he said. "Soon new people will come into this land and they will need those fish for food." Saying that, he turned the two women into birds. "See this day what I have done to you? Thus shall I call you Swallows. When the first salmon come, people will see swallows flying above the river and they will run to the banks to see White Salmon."

The birds soared and swooped above him, their forked tails silhouetted against the sun, as they called, "Pit-vik. Pit-vik."

"Thus did Coyote do it," Tsagaglalal said as she finished the story.

"So I did," Coyote agreed. Coyote's upper lip slipped back over yellow teeth into a satisfied smile. "It will be me, Coyote, the People will thank for bringing food to them."

Coyote pointed at the sky. "See! Even now swallows fly overhead and the fishermen of your village are watching the river for signs that White Salmon returns."

Her eyes searched the sky until she sighted the birds circling over the water. "There are other signs. I hear the cry of the dove," she said. "That also is a sign that now is the time for White Salmon to visit us again. I teach my people the signs."

Coyote growled deep in this throat. "Your people should remember they once could not eat the very fish they caught."

"My grandmother did say our people once were without mouths." A smile flickered across the face of Tsagaglalal. "She said it is because of Coyote some people have sad or sour looks on their faces."

Coyote harumphed. "My flint may have slipped once or twice. It was a very long day and I had grown tired."

Tsagaglalal did not want to offend powerful Coyote. "I did not mean. . . ."

"You make me lose my patience, woman. Who are you to dare talk thus to Coyote?"

"One who would like to hear the story from you," she said in a voice meant to soothe him. "Tell it to me as it happened."

He rumbled and growled and finally told this story as he turned and pointed his sharp nose toward the hill behind the ridge where they stood.

EARLY THAT MORNING, I was resting among the rocks up there. I bid goodnight to Moon and waited for Sun to light up Wy'east, our great mountain to the south and west. As the sky grew lighter, I started down the hill. Hunger gnawed at my belly. I searched for a ground squirrel or even a mouse to eat.

As I picked my way down the hill, over these very rocks, and walked down toward the river, a whiff of smoke curled up to meet me. A campfire. Perhaps food was cooking. I crept along to some bushes and peered out between the leaves. What did I see but a man coming up out of the water, pulling behind him a sturgeon, one as long as the man was tall. He dragged it up onto the bank and dived back down into the river. While he was under the water, I crept forward and pulled the big sturgeon back to the bushes and hid it and myself as well.

When the man came up out of the river, he was hauling another sturgeon behind him. He looked at the spot where the first sturgeon had been. When he saw it was gone, he put down the second one and set about looking for the first. This man pointed his finger up high, then a little lower and again lower still. Then he pointed to where I, Coyote, was crouching behind the bush. I tried to move this way and that to avoid the finger pointing at me, but no matter which way I turned, the finger pointed directly at me.

So I, Coyote, came out of the bushes and faced this man. When I came closer, I saw he had no mouth. What a strange looking man! He had eyes and a nose and two ears, but no mouth at all. This man made some sounds through his nose, "Den, den, den, den." Of course I did not understand him, because he had no mouth to turn the sounds into words. But I could see that his heart was dark with anger.

8

I asked myself, what if this person tries to kill me for taking his sturgeon? But the man only scowled at me and turned back to his canoe. While he was gone, I stirred up the campfire on the river bank. I cut up the sturgeon and made ready the stones. I laid the sturgeon out on hot stones and steamed it until it was done. I took the pieces of fish and laid them out on big leaves. Then that same man came back and watched as I ate. I lifted up a piece so he could see its juice drip. I chomped this delicious sturgeon down and licked up the juice. As I ate, I watched to see what the man would do.

The man took a piece of that good, well-done sturgeon. He sniffed deeply of the sturgeon, then threw the piece away.

"That is not the way to eat food," I told him. The man ignored me and grabbed another piece. He inhaled again and, as before, he threw the piece away.

I went up to this man and looked closely. I shall give him a mouth, I thought to myself. I took a flint out of my pouch. Then I drew close to him. The man dodged from side to side, but I pulled him to the ground. I ran the flint across his face and sliced open the place where his mouth should be. Blood flowed out of this new mouth. He gasped and snorted and twisted himself away from me. "Go to the river," I said to him, "and wash yourself."

When he had come up out of the water, the blood had stopped and he spoke to me in anger. "You have stolen my large sturgeon." Then he began to shake, for he realized he had spoken for the first time. His mouth turned up in a huge smile.

"Here, take some of this sturgeon and eat it in the proper way," I told him. He did, and he smacked his new lips.

Tsagaglalal nodded. "My grandmother said none of the people in his village had mouths and they were jealous of the man who came back with a mouth and who could eat instead of just smelling food. They called upon you, Coyote, to make mouths for all of them."

"And so I did." he said and went on with his story.

I traveled along the river until I reached his village. The people there rushed up to see the man's new mouth. The sounds of the people rose up in the village. "Nnn . . . nnn . . . nnn." Everywhere I turned I heard, "Nnn . . .nnn . . . nnn." They snorted and pointed to their faces. I felt sorry for them, so I went about the village, cutting a mouth for each child, each man and woman and each elder in the village. They all began to speak at once. Then some of them sang and laughed and a few cried out loud—all for the very first time.

"A good thing for you to do," Tsagaglalal said, mindful to give him full credit.

"True. But these people complained. Some said their mouths were too big, and some turned down as if the people were angry or sad."

"Some of them turned up at the corners into beautiful smiles," she reminded him.

E NOUGH OF THIS," Coyote said. "Go. Walk through your village. I will see how your people feel about what Coyote has given them. And I will watch you to see what kind of chief you are."

Tsagaglalal, anxious to show Coyote how well her people lived and how much they needed her, led the way down the narrow trail that fell in a steep drop between the boulders. As they descended, they heard shouts from below. The youth, Me'nait, who had led Coyote to Tsagaglalal, ran from the river bank to the cluster of longhouses in the clearing.

"Itkla'uwan! White Salmon! Our brothers and sisters in the river have returned," the youth shouted. "I, Me'nait, have seen the first fish of the fall run."

Tsagaglalal hastened to join her people. Great excitement spread up and down the river when the first salmon of the fall season was seen. Much depended on their catching many fish, for there would not be another such good run of salmon until the following spring. As she walked briskly through the tall, dry grass, she realized Coyote was no longer behind her.

She looked back up to the rocks. Although she could not see him, she felt him there, watching.

As she came into the village, Tsagaglalal saw Me'nait calling the people to greet Itkla'uwan, their friend in the river, who gave them food in such abundance. As the first to see the return of the salmon, Me'nait would be the first netter to mount one of the fishing platforms built of trunks and branches of sturdy fir trees. And he would be honored that night around the campfire.

The fishing platforms were built out over the water near the the falls. Here the river was compressed into a narrow channel. The torrent roared over massive pillars of shiny black basalt and white water frothed on the rapids below. From early spring until fall, in five or more runs, the salmon came up the river. In a silver flurry, shining salmon struggled against the current, arching up the rapids, rock by rock, toward the streams where they were born, to spawn and to die. The circle of their lives then complete.

Tsagaglalal thought of Coyote watching, watching. He must see how well her people lived. She stopped at the first cedar plank house. "Gather together your dip-nets and your long-handled spears," she said to the men there. "We must be ready to capture these mighty fish."

"Bring your baskets," she told a group of women she met along the path. "We will have many fish to dry and store away."

Dried fish meant more than food to the Wishram. Baskets of salmon were also highly prized by tribes who lived far away from the river. To trade for this delicacy, strangers traveled many miles to bring their goods to the villages on the banks of the Great River. Tribes along the Pacific Ocean bartered shells and seafood for the salmon. Plateau tribes to the east brought buffalo hides and pemmican, made from dried meat, berries and fat. Tribes from the north brought soft elk skins and woven blankets made of goat hair.

The river people, known as some of the best traders of the Northwest, lived well when they were successful in catching and drying salmon. Tsagaglalal urged her people on, exhorting them not to become lazy just because they lived amid such plenty.

TSAGAGLALAL STOOD ON THE RIVER BANK at the base of a fishing platform. A swirling mist hovered over the river and showered Me'nait with a soft spray as he claimed the honor of being the first netter to climb to the top. He looked at the platform which had seemed so sturdy when they lashed the fir logs and planks together, but which now seemed so high and slight a place to hold men above the white water far below.

"See how brave Me'nait is," Chief Tsagaglalal called out as he climbed the sides and pulled himself onto the platform. Before he leaned out over the water, he tied a rope of hemp securely about his waist.

Tsagaglalal remembered a time when Me'nait's younger brother slipped and fell from a platform such as this into the swirling water. In a quick swoop of his great net, a man had plucked the boy from the river, else he would have surely died. Over the years many brave fishermen had fallen to their deaths in the rapids below. Their spirits beckoned to Me'nait, but he was young and strong, and she could see he did not intend to follow them into the river. He would think only of the glory of netting the first salmon.

Then, far below, a splendid salmon whipped its body from side to side, its thrashing tail throwing it up over one rock and then another. Me'nait leaned out over the rapids, squinted his eyes against the spray, plunged his long-handled net under the fish and jerked it upward. Itkla'uwan struggled, flipping its body about wildly, but Me'nait held it in the net. Slowly he raised it up and brought the first catch onto the platform. Above the roar of the falling water, he heard the yells of the Wishram on the bank, cheering his victory.

Chief Tsagaglalal stepped forward to take the fish from Me'nait. The first salmon of the season would be steamed in a cooking pit over hot rocks. The chief and the elders, the old men and women of the village, would each eat a portion. Small pieces would be given to the children. Then the Wishram would drink deeply of cold water from the river as they had been taught to do. Me'nait would dive deep into an eddy at the base of the falls and leave the bones from this fish to insure that its brothers and sisters would return in the spring. The fishing post where Me'nait caught the fish would thus be made lucky.

Other men of the village climbed the platforms and swooped great numbers of salmon into their nets or lined the bank of the river below the falls and plunged their spears into flailing fish. The elders gathered near the fishermen. If a netter quietly put a fish down on the platform, an elder would come

forward, kill the fish and tap it, and show which villager could step forward and claim it. If the fisherman slapped his thigh, though, those below would know he was keeping the fish for his own family, and they would continue squatting on the bank. Thus did all the families share in the bounty.

14

A S THE PEOPLE WENT ABOUT THEIR WORK, the clouds of
morning gave way to a brilliant blue sky. "You have done well,"
Tsagaglalal told the fishermen. "Our people will have a good winter." She
looked about her. She did not catch sight of Coyote, but she knew he would
see and would surely be impressed.

Then began the hard work of preparing the fish. The women cut apart the salmon and put them on racks made of green alder branches until they had dried. Tsagaglalal wondered if Coyote would still be in the village when the women prepared the dried fish for trading. They would pound the red-orange strips of flesh with stones until they were flaked into a powder. Then the women would bring deep bags, woven of cedar roots and rushes, each at least an arm's length long. The women lined the bags with salmon skin and pressed in the dried salmon flour. In other baskets, they packed smoked sides of salmon. Then they tightly laced the tops with cords of hemp. They covered the bags with grass mats and stacked them in great piles. Tsagaglalal tested the bags to be sure each was ready. "We will have food to eat all winter long, and much to trade," she said. "None will go hungry before White Salmon comes again in the spring."

A NEWI'KUS, A GRANDMOTHER, brought Tsagaglalal a bowl carved out of wood. "Eat, our chief. I have made a broth of salmon flakes flavored with dried mountain huckleberries." Tsagaglalal ate with great relish, showing Coyote how well her people fed her.

The stately chief passed among her people, encouraging their preparations for winter. Some pushed moss into the cracks between the planks to protect those within from the cold East Wind that would soon press the cold inside. Five longhouses made of fir logs and cedar planks made up the permanent village. As many as thirty people worked and ate and slept in each one. Children and old ones gathered firewood for fires that would be needed for cooking, and for sitting about on long winter nights when they would tell tales of Coyote and of Eagle and of White Salmon.

Tsagaglalal went to the river and watched men prepare canoes for winter. Each canoe was made from a trunk of a cedar tree gouged out wide in the middle and tapered at each end. High prows were carved with figures telling of adventures on the river. The Wishram canoes rode high on the water and could carry the immense burden of bales of pressed salmon down river for trade. "You have done well," Tsagaglalal told the men.

The day drew to a close. The people returned to their houses. Salmon splayed on sticks leaned in toward a campfire being made ready for the evening meal. Still there was no sign of Coyote. As Tsagaglalal walked about the village, she pushed away a feeling of dread that had pressed on her heart all day.

The mists of evening began to gather. Tsagaglalal walked along the trail that led to the special place in the rocks that was her own. Dry golden grasses brushed her legs as she crossed a meadow at the base of the rocks. There she came upon a cluster of small children playing a game with pebbles in the dust. "Come to me," she said, as she sat down on a fallen tree. "I will tell you stories of our people so you may remember them long after I am gone and you will tell them to your children."

They sat down around her feet and waited for her to begin. "What do you see out there?" she asked.

The littlest girl looked out across the river where the setting sun had turned the water into melted gold. A band of shimmering colors arched over the mist from the falls. "A rainbow," she cried. "I see a rainbow."

"It is so," said the chief. Tsagaglalal smiled and leaned forward to pat the little girl's hand. Then she looked around at the others. "And what does the rainbow tell us?"

The tallest boy, standing behind the little ones, said, "It can mean good or bad."

"You are right. These are the signs, for those of us who dwell along the river. My grandmother told me that where the rainbow falls to earth, a baby will be born. Sometimes, though, we see a bad rainbow. If it is summer, this means that Sun will be strong; he will sting and burn and no rain will fall to make the grasses green. If we see a good rainbow, then the weather will be fine and Sun will refresh us. Just so in winter; snow will fall when Rainbow is bad, West Wind will bring sheets of freezing rain, or East Wind will blow snow and ice that will cover the rocks. But if one sees a good rainbow, we will not have hardship even though it be winter."

"I don't understand. How will we know if the rainbow is good or bad?" the little girl asked.

"You will not always know, but as you grow older and wiser, you will watch all the signs from Rainbow and Sun and Moon. Listen to the howls of East Wind and the whispers of West Wind. You will come to understand

what they say to you. Now look at Moon coming up over the rocks above us. How do the old ones say to act toward her?"

They looked at the full moon, the color of a honeycomb from a bear tree, which had slipped up above the bluff behind them as evening darkened into night. They shook their heads. They had not heard this tale of the big harvest moon.

"When Moon shines very brightly, as she does tonight, we Wishram go out of our longhouses and walk along the river. Plainly is she seen, but we are careful never to point her out to one another with our fingers. It is a bad thing to do and will cause a great frost to take place. Moon will become ashamed if you point at her."

"There is so much to know," one child complained.

"Not too much, for you are very clever. Be ever watchful for these signs. You must learn them well," Tsagaglalal told them.

A girl almost as tall as the chief stood and looked toward the river. "Look, Chief Tsagaglalal. The moon makes stars dance on the water."

"Tell us the story of stars on the water," a little boy said.

She smiled at him. "Your grandmothers and grandfathers have told you this story many times."

"Again," the children said. "Tell it again."

"Just so," Chief Tsagaglalal said and she began the story of why stars float on Great River.

ONCE, FIVE YOUNG MAIDENS FROM THE VILLAGE came to this very meadow. The night was warm and they came here to stay the night. They looked at the sky as they waited for sleep to come. The eldest pointed out the largest star. "I should like to have that star for a husband," she said.

Another pointed. "I should like to have that one."

The youngest said, "I should like to have that one," pointing to the smallest. "Mine is the prettiest," she said, "although it is dim and small." Finally, after each one had chosen, they talked about their stars until they fell into a deep sleep.

That night, all five stars came down to earth. This was when stars were the same as people and could go anywhere they wished. The five star men asked the five maidens to be their wives. The star men came to their wives in this field each night as darkness fell and left again each morning before sunrise, as they had been told they must. The star that had looked the smallest was in reality the oldest and largest of them all. Once, just before dawn, four of the star people left for the sky, but the big one was tired and stayed there in the meadow, asleep, with the young women. When Sun stroked the cheeks of the women and caused them to wake, they saw the youngest of them lying beside a gray-haired old man. The women were frightened and ran away.

Thus did our people find out stars were coming down to earth at night, and the stars in the sky vowed never to visit earth again. The old star man **in the meadow could no longer return to the sky so he turned himself into a**

21

bright, white rock on the river bank where he could be seen by all the tribes. This village became a great gathering place for all those who lived near. Every one knew of the Star Rock and knew of the Wishram who came to be called the Star People.

"What happened next?" Chief Tsagaglalal asked them.

"I know," a little boy cried out. "The Wasco people across the river saw the good luck Star Rock brought to our village."

"It was so and it made them angry," she said. "They waited until they saw our people leave to gather berries in a mountain meadow. Some Wasco men crossed the river in their mighty canoes and went to Star Rock. They pushed and pulled, but the rock did not move. They signaled other men to cross the river and help them. Finally, with a great push, they rolled it into the water."

The chief looked about her. "So, young ones, what did our grandfathers do then?"

"Our people came back to the village and saw Star Rock was gone."

A little girl wiggled in excitement. "They searched and searched and they didn't find it."

The chief nodded. "That is true. And then they were angry. They looked for signs and saw that the Wasco had come and had done something to Star Rock.

Our people crossed the river in their canoes and accused the Wasco," the chief said. "Wasco means those who have a big cup, and so they did. Into that huge rock cup flowed pure cold water from a spring above their village. The Wasco people were very proud of it. Our Wishram people knew how they could repay the Wasco. While the elders argued, a few Wishram men slipped away and found the huge cup rock. Our men beat that rock with sticks until it broke and only a small part of it was left.

In time, the neighbors from the south bank and the north bank of Great River made peace with each other. But, as the years passed, the Wishram were no longer called the Star People."

"But we did find the Star Rock again, didn't we?" the little girl asked.

"Yes, but not right away," Tsagaglalal said. "Spring Sun, though not as mighty as Summer Sun, had melted snow from the sides of Wy'east, the great mountain south of the two villages. The river was full to the top of its banks. But when autumn came again, and the water in the river was low, what did our people see?"

"Pieces of Star Rock!"

"And what happened to Star Rock?" the children asked, though they knew the story very well.

"Star Rock had shattered into many pieces and each one makes a tiny star on the water when the moon shines," she finished.

"Another story. Another," the children begged.

But Tsagaglalal rose from her place on the rock and sent the children back to their lodges. Tsagaglalal returned to her place on top of the rocks to watch over the Wishram and dream dreams of happiness and prosperity for them. It was the tenth month, the Travels-in-Canoes Moon, and early darkness settled over her. She had not seen Coyote in the village that day. Perhaps it was as she wished and he had gone away.

In the distance, from the hills behind her back, she heard, "Ah-hoo-o-o. Ah-hoo-o-o. Ah-hoo-o-o."

From another hilltop came an answer, and then another. Coyote must be nearby. "If you are here, reveal yourself. Did you see how many fish my people took from the river? Did you see the preparations they make for winter?"

A stick snapped behind her. "I am here," a voice said, still muffled by the bearskin robe. "I, Coyote, have seen. Is it not I who has brought such abundance to your people? And I who have taught them how to do these things?"

"It is so, but not all that Coyote does is so grand," Tsagaglalal told him. She reminded him of his greediness and the way he played tricks on the People, and how, sometimes, the jokes were played back on him. "The People tell another tale of Coyote."

"Tell me what they say of me."

"I will tell you," she answered, and she began this story:

EAST WIND BLEW DRIFTS OF SNOW that covered the land in one of the worst winters in many years. Coyote was hungry. He ran down to Great River where Fish-Hawk, one of the Old Ones, and his wife dwelled. "Grandson," he said to Fish-Hawk, for he spoke to him with that title of respect, "will you not give me something to eat?"

Although Fish-Hawk and his wife gave him much food, Coyote still was not satisfied. Then they gave him food five times more. At last they lost their patience. "When are you going home?" they asked him.

"Oh, soon," Coyote said, not worried that he was eating up the food they had stored for the rest of the long winter.

Fish-Hawk said, "Come down to the river with me."

There Coyote saw a tall stump by the water, and a hole in the ice that had opened up near the bank. Fish-Hawk gave a fierce cry, jumped onto the stump and from there he arched himself high above the ice and dove through the hole in the ice. Coyote became terribly frightened and ran around crying, "My grandson is drowning! My grandson is drowning!"

But soon Fish-Hawk came out through the hole with five different kinds of fish and gave them to Coyote, thinking this would satisfy him and that he would go away. And so Coyote did.

Then, as the days passed and he grew hungry again, Coyote remembered how well he ate at the house of Fish-Hawk, so he went back there. "Come to the river with me," Fish-Hawk said to him again. When they reached the river, Coyote walked over and climbed up on the stump near the ice-hole as he had seen Fish-Hawk do. Fish-Hawk smiled and wondered what Coyote would do next. Coyote began to shout as Fish-Hawk had done. Then Coyote leaped up into the air, just as Fish-Hawk had done, and dove toward the hole in the ice. Alas, he missed the hole, hit his head upon the ice and was stunned.

It was some time before he came to his senses. About evening Coyote recovered and the wife of Fish-Hawk helped him up. He left there, as angry as he could be. News of his foolishness spread to every village along the river.

As she finished the story, Tsagaglalal stood tall. "Is that not Coyote, also?" she asked.

Coyote pulled back deeper into the shadows of the rocks. He was not pleased to be reminded of his foolishness, but he could not deny his greediness had often brought him to grief. He muttered, "It is so. I have done such things." Then his voice grew louder. "But I also lead the People and tell them how things will be. When your people were new along the river, they did not know all the ways of living. Was it not I, Coyote, who taught them how to gather roots and berries, how to use the spear and the net to catch White Salmon? Did they not learn how to clothe themselves in the skins of Elk and Deer? Did they not learn from me how to make fine lodges of cedar and fir? It was Coyote who taught them the songs and the stories of the Old Ones."

"It is so," the chief said.

The cold wind once again touched Tsagaglalal's face and the chief grew increasingly wary. Coyote did indeed do great things for her people, but what did he plan for them now? Tsagaglalal counseled herself to remain calm. Coyote was also known to bluff his way through a situation. Perhaps this was such a time.

She willed her voice to remain strong to show him her courage. "Why do you seek me out? What has Coyote to do with me?"

"I come to tell you of changes."

"I have heard that Coyote can tell the future."

He growled low in his throat in a way that caused dread in her heart. "I can tell you of some things I know will happen."

"And what are those things?" she asked.

"First let me ask you, Chief Tsagaglalal, what kind of living do you give these people? Do you treat them well, or are you an evil woman?"

"You have seen me. I teach them to live well. You can see the strong lodges we have built. My people can show you many things strangers bring to barter for our salmon. But, more than that, I teach them to do good. I do much for my people and they are loyal to me."

"I have seen that it is so," Coyote told her. "Even so, I am here to tell you the world is soon going to change. New people will come and life on the river will be different. There will be a great sickness. Many deaths. Life will not be the same along the river." He leaned forward and the bearskin slipped back off his shoulders. She saw the sharp outline of his head as he stepped out of the shadow.

"Even if it is as you say, what do these things have to do with me?"

He leaned close to her. "You, woman, will no longer lead the Wishram. You will no longer be a chief. Indeed, there will be no more women chiefs. As for you, the time has come for you to join your grandparents."

She drew herself up. "I will be the chief of my people as long as they desire me to lead them."

His growl grew deeper. "You can tell the future then?"

"I cannot tell the future, but in my heart I know my people. I know they are just and they will not forsake me. If I have become wise in my years as chief, I do not need to tell the future. I will not walk away from my people even if you say it must be so. Come again with me and we will go among them. See how well they live. See that I am not an evil woman."

"I have walked among them, and what you say is true. Still, I say you will not be chief as the sun rises tomorrow."

"If you cause me to die, my people will mourn me. The women will cut off their long hair. They will rub black ashes on their faces. They will cover me with a woven cloth and decorate me with shell beads and bracelets. They will carry me in honor to the burial vault and place me there among the dead. They will return to the village and will walk in darkness for ten days and five days more.

Coyote growled. "Your time at this place is at an end, but since you desire it, you will not be separated from your people."

He raised his voice into a command. "Stay here and watch over the people who will live at this place. Your name, Tsagaglalal, shall mean She Who Watches, and you will guard over your people for all the years to come. This I tell you will be so."

Coyote slipped away in the darkness and was not seen by the Wishram again.

CHIEF TSAGAGLALAL HAD DISAPPEARED. Although her people became alarmed when she did not return to the village, and ran up through the rocks looking for her, they could find no sign of her. They saw only the strange new face carved on the pillar of rock, which stared at them with large, knowing eyes. Me'nait and the others searched for Tsagaglalal for many days, up and down the river banks and on the bluffs above, but they never found her. She was mourned for many moons.

People of the village and their grandchildren in all the generations to follow, came to stand before the haunting face carved on the rock, and they held it in great reverence. Tales were told of Coyote and Tsagaglalal.

People knew that "She Who Watches" sees all things, for whenever they looked up at the stone carving, her large eyes followed them. Those who came to the rock to see her face were reminded to do good and to live well.

Now those who climb onto the very rocks her feet once stepped upon, back in the mists of time, stand and look at that knowing face and those penetrating eyes.

So do good and live well. She watches.

Epilogue

COYOTE WAS RIGHT. Much has changed. A Wishram prophecy that new people, white people, would come to live by the river came true. Explorers Lewis and Clark visited the village in 1806. Traders from England and France and the new country, the United States of America, brought goods to trade up and down the Columbia River and left diseases behind which killed many, many thousands of the river people. Soon new settlers arrived over what became known as the Oregon Trail. Not far below the falls at the village of Nixlu'idix, these pioneers could choose between a dangerous overland trail or the equally frightening trip down the Columbia River. The daring pioneers who chose the river way, tied their covered wagons onto log rafts and challenged the remaining rapids. Though a number of them were swept away and drowned in the turbulent river, most lived through this experience and continued on to claim homesteads in the fertile valleys beyond.

The roaring torrent of water that plunged down Celilo Falls over huge rocks in the narrows between Nixlu'idix and the Wasco village is no more. In 1957, The Dalles Dam was finished and the frantic rapids of the Columbia River were forever tamed. Water spreads out behind John Day Dam, The Dalles Dam and Bonneville Dam turning this middle stretch of the river into immense lakes moving forward over spillways toward the sea. A constant surge of water goes through the turbines at the dams and makes electricity for the Northwest and beyond.

Most members of the Wishram band were relocated to the Yakima Reservation in south central Washington. Many Columbia River Indians did not want to leave their homes along the river, even though their fishing grounds were changed forever. Some acquired homesteads after the homestead laws were amended in 1884 to allow them to do so. A few lived along the river on land purchased by the federal government

31

for them to replace fishing sites inundated by Bonneville Dam. Other Native Americans spurned the treaties they did not want and continued to live on their traditional home places along the river. But the village of Nixlu'idix is no more.

The silver ribbons of salmon that came in seemingly endless numbers to give Indians of the river food to eat and food to trade are now in such limited supply that some runs are being called endangered. Far fewer fish make it up the fish ladders of the dams than fought their way over the rapids of Wi'mahl, the Great River. Commercial fishermen, sports fishermen and Native Americans all feel that their shares of small runs are in peril. Salmon hatcheries that attempt to supplant natural spawning are not making up numbers lost.

What changes does the petroglyph, "She Who Watches," see as she looks out over the Columbia River? Directly below her, railroad tracks run along the top of a levee built against potential flooding. To her left, on the land where the village of the Wishram people once stood, is a Washington state park with camp sites for recreational vehicles and picnic places on broad green lawns. The site has been named a Registered National Historical Place in honor of Nixlu'idix.

Out on the broad river-lake in front of her, a tug pushes two bargeloads of grain toward the locks in the dams on its way down river toward Portland and the grain elevators there. Sailboats and motor boats skim over the water. The friendly West Wind of summer flits sail boarders back and forth across choppy water like butterflies fluttering from petal to petal.

On the south side of the river, on U.S. I-84, cars, motor homes, trucks and buses speed along the transcontinental highway. On tracks next to the highway, trains rumble from the west coast to the east coast. Overhead, jets carry as many people on each flight as ever lived at one time in the village below.

As Coyote predicted, there have been many changes. However, Coyote did not prevent other Native American women in other places from becoming leaders of their people.

One thing has not changed. "She Who Watches" continues to gaze out across the water as the guardian of the Columbia Gorge, exhorting people: Do good and live well.

She watches.

Author's Notes

The ancient petroglyph of "She Who Watches" is scratched onto a dark reddish-gray slab of rock not far above the north shore of the Columbia River, just east of The Dalles Dam. The haunting face is nearly as tall as a grown woman and as wide as her outstretched arms. It is unusual, perhaps unique in the Northwest, because it links ancient rock art with a legend told by a band of Native Americans, the Wishram, a few of whom still live nearby. The Wishram band of Chinook Indians is one of many Native American groups who have lived for many thousands of years in what are now the states of Washington and Oregon. Archaeologists have found signs of habitation along the river believed to go back at least 10,000 years.

Many of the legends and customs of the Wishram in this book come from direct translations of the very difficult Wishram language, and from other interviews in the early 1900s with the "oldest of the old" of the Wishram and Wasco people who lived along the river. In his ethnological study, *Wishram Texts*, Edward Sapir wrote of the methods he used:

> "The material . . . was obtained for the most part, in Yakima Reservation, situated in southern Washington, in July and August of 1905 . . . taking down Indian text all in strictly phonetic shape and published here with such comparatively slight revision as they seemed to demand." The translation from Wishram into English was done by Pete McGuff, "a younger generation of Indian . . . a half-blood (his father was a Negro, his mother is a full-blood Indian.)"

33

McGuff lived much of his life with the Wishram and spoke their language fluently. Sapir continues:

> "The bulk of the material . . . was dictated by Louis Simpson, Indian name Me'nait."

Me'nait was, at that time, about seventy-five years old, placing his date of birth about 1830. The stories from his childhood, therefore, drew on memories from before the westward march of the white settlers on the Oregon Trail or the removal of most of the Wishram band to the Yakima Reservation in the 1880s. Me'nait is used as the name for the young netter of fish in this story, and, whenever possible, words directly from the Wishram translations were used.

Descriptions of the clothing, baskets and the village of Nixlu'idix and other settlements of the time along the river come from *Columbia River Baskets*, also *Wishram Ethnography* and the portion of *The Journals of Lewis and Clark* written in October of 1805. Captain William Clark wrote of the canoes described in this story:

> "Capt. (Meriweather) Lewis went up to the Lodges to See those Canoes and exchanged our Smallest canoe for one of them by giving a Hatchet & few trinkets . . . these canoes are neeter made than any I have ever Seen and calculated to ride the waves, and carry emence burthens."

Stories about the petroglyph selected for this book all come from legends connected with "She Who Watches." Other interpretations have been made of the petroglyphs. James D. Keyser, in his book, *Indian Rock Art of the Columbia Plateau*, tells of shamanistic and death cult rituals related to them. It is estimated that as many as eighty percent of the Native Americans in the region died in the early 1800s of measles, small pox and other diseases to which they had no resistance, and which were brought by explorers, traders and settlers.